PSYCHOANALYSIS
for Teachers and Parents

PSYCHOANALYSIS
for Teachers and Parents

INTRODUCTORY LECTURES BY
ANNA FREUD

TRANSLATED BY

BARBARA LOW

AUTHOR OF "PSYCHOANALYSIS:
AN OUTLINE OF THE FREUDIAN THEORY"

W · W · NORTON & COMPANY

NEW YORK · LONDON

First published as a Norton paperback 1979 by arrangement with Emerson Books, Inc.

W. W. Norton & Company, Inc. is also the publisher of the works of Erik H.
Erikson, Otto Femchel, Karen Horney, Harry Stack Sullivan, and The Standard
Edition of the Complete Psychological Works of Sigmund Freud.

Library of Congress Cataloging in Publication Data

Freud, Anna, 1895-
Psychoanalysis for teachers and parents.
Translation of Einführung in die Psychoanalyse
für Pädagogen.
Reprint of the ed. published by Emerson Books,
New York.
Includes index.
1. Child analysis.   2. Educational psy-
chology.   I. Title.
[LB1051.F84813   1979]   370.15   78–25954
ISBN   0–393–00918–1 pbk.

1 2 3 4 5 6 7 8 9 0

These four lectures were given be-fore the teachers at the Children's Centers of the City of Vienna.

Contents

PSYCHOANALYSIS
for Teachers and Parents

LECTURE I

Infantile Amnesia and the Oedipus Complex

We are all aware that practical teachers are still very suspicious and doubtful of psychoanalysis. When, therefore, in spite of this, you Hort teachers of Vienna * determined to have a short course of lectures from me, you must somehow or other have received the impression that a closer acquaintance with this new science might be able to afford you some help

* The word *Hort* has been left in German, as it appears likely to mislead if an English substitute were attempted. A quotation from an account of a Hort has been included by way of explanation: "The Hort is a kind of kindergarten, but particularly for children from six to fourteen years of age. The kindergarten itself only takes children up to six years or until school age. The children who come to the Hort are the children of parents who go out to work. They come daily and return to their parents in the evening. Here, in the Hort, they prepare their school homework, occupy themselves with light work or communal games, and are taken for outings by the Hort workers."

in your difficult work. After you have listened to the four lectures you will be able to decide whether you were very wide of the mark in this supposition, or whether I have been able to fulfill at least some of your expectations.

In one particular direction I have certainly nothing new to offer you. I should fail in my object if I attempted to tell you anything about the behavior of schoolchildren and children of these centers, since you are in this respect in a most advantageous position. An immense amount of material passes through your hands in your daily work, and teaches you to recognize very clearly the whole range of the phenomena before you: from the physically and mentally retarded children, the obstinate, cowed, lying and ill-treated children, to the brutal, aggressive and delinquent ones. It is better not to attempt to give you a complete list, for you might well point out to me a large number of omissions.

But the very situation that gives you such a complete knowledge of these phenomena has its drawbacks. You are obliged, as the educators of the children of these Horts—just as you were as teachers in the schools and in the kindergarten—ceaselessly to *act*. The life and movement in your classes or groups demand constant interference on your part; you are obliged to admonish, discipline, keep in order, employ, advise, and instruct the children. The authorities above you would be greatly dissatisfied if it suddenly occurred to you to withdraw to the position of a passive observer. Thus it comes about that in the practice of your profession you become acquainted with numberless visible manifestations of childish behavior, but you are unable to arrange systematically the phenomena before your eyes, nor can you trace to their original source the manifestations of the children on whom, however, you are bound to react.

Perhaps even more than the opportunity for undisturbed observation you lack the power to make a right classification and explanation of the material you possess, for such a classification demands very special knowledge. Let us assume for the moment that one of you among my audience is specially interested in finding out why certain children in a particular group suffer from inflamed eyes or rickets. He knows that these children come from miserable, damp homes, but only medical knowledge can explain clearly to him the special way in which the dampness of the walls in the home causes the child's illness. Another of you, perhaps, concentrates his attention on the dangers to which the children of drunkards are exposed owing to their inheritance; in this case he must study the teachings of heredity. Whoever wishes to discover the connection between unemployment, the housing shortage, and neglected children must try to get some insight into sociology. But the teacher who desires to learn more of the mental background of all the phenomena of which I have told you earlier, and who would like to understand the differences between them and follow their slow development in the case of the individual child, may very possibly obtain information through the new science of psychoanalysis.

Any such assistance in practical work through increased knowledge seems to me of

special importance to the workers in these
Horts for two reasons. The Children's Hort,
which is obliged to receive all children exposed to various dangers in and out of their
parents' homes in the intervals when they are
not at school, is the youngest of the municipal
educational institutions of the City of Vienna.
The Children's Hort is regarded as the rem-
edy for the growing neglect of children. It
owes its existence to the belief that in the
earlier stages of neglect and asocial behavior a
beneficial influence is best exercised in the
Hort which is close to, and yet free from, the
school or parental environment. It is felt that
it is much more difficult to do this later by iso-
lating in reformatories the long-neglected or
criminal adolescents, who are then too often
beyond any educational experiments. But at
present there is no compulsory attendance at
the Hort. The authorities can compel the parents to send their children to the schools to be
taught, but whether they will entrust to the
Hort a child to whom they can give at home
only the worst of conditions is, at present, a
matter for the parents' own judgment. Hence

it follows that the Children's Hort must constantly justify its existence to each child and to its parents by especially successful work, just as, before the introduction of compulsory vaccination, parents had to be again and again convinced of the necessity for inoculation.

But the worker at the Child Hort has another special difficulty inherent in his position. He has to deal almost exclusively with children who have already had a whole series of more or less profound experiences and who have passed through the hands of numbers of educators. He must note that these children, at any rate at first, do not in the least react to his real individuality and to his actual behavior toward them. They simply bring with them a preconceived attitude of mind, and may approach the teacher with the suspicion, defiance, or feeling of having to be on guard which they have acquired through their personal experience of other adults. Moreover, the life of the child in the Children's Hort is only supplementary to his school life, and the Hort generally adopts methods more liberal, humane, and modern than prevail in most schools. Thus it happens that the standard of behavior which the school demands from, and inculcates into, the children often proves a hindrance to the Hort in the attainment of its own aims.

The position of the worker in the Child Hort is, therefore, by no means enviable. In almost every case he has a difficult task before him which requires independent action and understanding, but unfortunately he comes late to the scene as coworker and educator.

But we should be unjust to the school if we were to estimate the position of the teacher there as more favorable than that of the Hort worker. As a matter of fact teachers complain that they seldom get the child at firsthand, and that it is very difficult, for example, to accustom the children in the first classes of the elementary schools to a correct and serious attitude toward the teacher and definite instruction, since until then they have lived in the play atmosphere of the kindergarten. They bring with them into the school the behavior acquired in the former, which is no longer suitable in the latter.

Yet when we turn to the kindergarten teachers who, according to the view just expressed, should be in the enviable position of dealing with untilled ground, we hear to our amazement the complaint that even the three-to-six-year-old children dealt with in the kindergarten are nothing but "ready-made men." Each child brings with him a collection of characteristics, and reacts to the behavior of the kindergarten teacher in his own precise fashion. There is to be discovered in each child a perfectly definite constellation of hopes and fears, dislikes and preferences, his own kind of jealousy and tenderness, and his need of love or his rejection of it. It is no question here of a teacher impressing her own individuality upon a still unformed being. She is moving among complex miniature personalities whom it is by no means easy to influence.

The teachers—whether in Child Horts, schools or kindergartens—are thus all placed in the same difficult position. Human beings obviously develop earlier than we generally imagine. In order to trace to their origins the

childish peculiarities which give these teachers so much trouble, investigations must ex-
tend to the period previous to the child's entrance into the educational institutions. They
must go back to those teachers who were actually the first ones in his life, that is, to the
period before his fifth year, and to his parents.

Perhaps it seems to you as if our task was
thereby simplified Instead of observing the
daily behavior of the older children in the
schools or in the Horts, we shall seek to
gather from them data concerning the impressions and remembrances of their earliest
years.

At first sight this does not appear a difficult
task. In your intercourse with the children entrusted to your care you have all tried to establish frank and honest relations between yourselves and the pupils. This will now be very
useful to you. The child will be prepared to
tell you everything if you will only begin to
question him.

I advise all of you to make this attempt,
but I can inform you in advance that it will
yield no results. Children give no information

about the past: they willingly talk about the events of the last few days or weeks, about holidays which they have spent in strange surroundings, about a former birthday or saint's day, perhaps even about the Christmas festivities of last year. But then their recollections come to a standstill, or at any rate they lack the power to impart them to others.

You will say, of course, we were too confident in our belief in the child's capacity to remember his past life. We ought to have borne in mind that the child draws no distinction between what is important and what unimportant in the past. It would therefore, you think, be much more reasonable and more fruitful of results to address such an inquiry concerning the earliest experiences of childhood, not to the child, but to the adult who is interested in such an investigation.

I certainly advise you to carry out this second suggestion, but I know you will be astonished to find that the friend to whom you apply and who is only too willing to help you has also very little to tell you. His recollections will apparently go back, with few gaps

and quite intelligently, to his fifth or sixth
year. He will describe his schooling, perhaps
even the houses where he lived in his third,
fourth, or fifth year, the number and names of
his brothers and sisters, and it may be some
such event as a removal from one house to
another, or some misfortune that happened.
Then his account will come to an end before
you have got at what you sought, namely, indications as to how his development during
those first years has resulted in his own individuality and his special characteristics.

But you must know that there is a reason
for this new disappointment. The events we
are searching for, which are called upon to
play so important a part in the development
of the particular individual's character, must
obviously be the most intimate events in his
life. They are experiences which a person
guards as his most private property, admitted
to himself alone and hidden as something
shameful from his dearest friends. We have to
reckon with this situation beforehand, and
apply for data to the only person who is in a
position to impart the information concern-

ing the whole state of affairs. That is to say, each investigator must investigate himself. We have, indeed, to rely upon the capacity of the normal adult to remember things, upon his interest in the investigation and upon his willingness to overthrow all those barriers, erected by a sense of shame, which prevent the revelation of himself to others. But even if we do give all our interest and all our attention to the matter and are as perfectly frank as we can be, the results will still be very poor. We shall not succeed in really elucidating the earliest years of our life and in collecting a complete series of recollections of that period. We shall certainly be able to string together incidents up to a certain point of time, which differs greatly in different individuals. With many it is the fifth year, with some the fourth, with others the third. Before that period there is for each a great blank, an abyss in which only single incidents torn from their connection are identified and on closer consideration appear to have no meaning and certainly no value. Perhaps, for example, a young man remembers nothing of the first four years of

his childhood except a brief scene on a ship
when the captain in a beautiful uniform
stretched out his arms to lift him over a little
parapet. Yet at that very time he had suffered
the stormiest conflicts and the most severe
blows of fate—as was easily ascertained by
questioning other people. Or again, a girl
who has had an emotional childhood, full of
vivid incidents, has retained nothing of it all
but the clear recollection of being taken out
in a perambulator and turning back her head
to look at her nurse who was pushing it!

You will grant that here we are up against
a startlingly contradictory set of facts. On the
one hand, we know from our observation of
little children, and from the accounts which
our relatives give us of our own childhood,
that the child behaves at this stage intelligently and energetically, shows likes and dislikes, and conducts himself in many important
respects quite like a rational being. On the
other hand, this period has vanished from his
own recollection, or perhaps has left behind it
only very incomplete traces. According to the
evidence given by educators, such as teachers

in schools and kindergartens, human beings after the expiration of these very early years step into life as completely formed little individualities. And yet memory acts as if .it were not worth while to preserve traces of a time in which each individual is capable of receiving quite special impressions and absorbing them, a time when this complex development has unfolded itself into an individuality.

The orthodox school of psychology has been deceived by this semblance of things. As the orthodox psychologists regard as material for their science only that part of the inner life of man which is known to the man himself, they must necessarily underestimate the significance of the first years of life, which remain unknown.

It was psychoanalysis that first tackled this contradiction. It was psychoanalysis that succeeded in proving that there was always at the root of the little daily mistakes of human beings—such as forgetfulness, losing things, various accidents, errors in reading, etc.— some purposive desire. Previously these oc-

currences had been explained without much
thought, as the results of lack of attention, of
fatigue or mere accident. Through psychoanalytic investigation of these mishaps it was
established that, generally speaking, we forget
nothing except what we wish to forget for
some good reason or other, a reason which
may, however, be quite unknown to our-
selves. Thus in the investigations into the gap
in childhood's memory, psychoanalysis will
not be content with the ordinary means of
elucidation. It assumes that such a striking
phenomenon could not have occurred without some very strong motive. It is just exactly
this obscurity, clouding the first years of life,
and the obstacles standing in the way of all
efforts to get at a direct elucidation, that
would make the psychoanalyst suspect something of importance was hidden there. In the
same way a burglar would conclude from a
specially elaborate safety lock on a safe which
was very difficult to pick that his efforts would
be well rewarded; people scarcely take so
much trouble to lock up something worth-
less!

But I have no intention of describing to you at present the way in which psychoanalysis has succeeded in its object of recovering the memories of childhood. The description of the psychoanalytic method would in itself claim far more time than we have at our disposal. We must leave a more detailed study and a further examination of this method of working for another course. At present we are chiefly interested in the content of the first years of childhood so far as psychoanalysis has succeeded in putting it together. This it has done, I must remind you, by explanation of the trivial mistakes already mentioned and of the dreams of healthy people, as well as by elucidation and analysis of the symptoms of the neurotic.

The psychoanalytic reconstruction of the childhood years extends as far back as infancy, when the child possesses only the inherited qualities which he brings with him at birth. The infant is thus in the state in which we erroneously hoped to find him on his entrance into the educational institutions. There is little creditable to report concerning this stage of his life. The tiny human being whom we have before us is extraordinarily like a new-born animal in all respects, except that he is in a worse position than the animal. The animals are dependent on the care of their mothers for only a short period, at most a few weeks. They then evolve into independent creatures who can get along without further care. It is quite different with human beings. The child remains for at least a year so completely dependent on its mother that it would perish immediately she withdrew her care. But even after the expiration of this year of infancy the child has not attained independence. It does not know how to procure its food, how to support itself, how to protect itself and ward off dangers of any kind. We know that the human being needs almost fifteen years before it can completely dispense with the protection of the grownups and become a grown-up individual.

This distinction between the human being and the animal, the child's long period of complete dependence, determines his entire destiny. As nothing stands between the child and destruction for the entire first year of his life except the tender care of his mother, we are not surprised if the maintenance of this maternal care begins to play a very important part in his life. The little child feels safe as long as he knows his mother is near at hand, and he shows his helplessness in a feeling of anguish when she has gone away from him. He needs his mother for the satisfaction of his hunger; she becomes a necessity of life. But the relationship between the infant and the mother soon goes far beyond what is to be explained as the striving for the preservation of his life. We note that the child wants his mother near him and longs for her when his hunger is satisfied and no special dangers threaten him. We say the child loves his mother. In response to her tender love and care a bond has been established with his mother which certainly still continues in line with the direction indicated by his instinct for self-preservation. But it has become quite independent of this instinct for self-preservation and goes far beyond it.

Because of this tender relation to his

mother it seems as if the little child would
have every chance of a peaceful physical and
mental development. He would be completely content if his mother did nothing but
feed him, take care of him, love him. But now
comes the moment when the external world,
for the first time, enters disturbingly into the
relation between the child and his mother.
The child who has now left his infancy and his
first year behind him suddenly learns that his
mother does not belong to him alone. The
family of which he is only a small and not a
very important part has other members—
father and brothers and sisters, of whose presence he has only just become aware, but who
appear just as important as he thinks himself.
They all, indeed, assert a right to the possession of the mother.

It can easily be understood that the small
child regards his brothers and sisters as his
enemies. He is jealous of them and wishes
them out of the way so as to restore the original state of affairs, which alone is satisfactory
to him.

You can convince yourselves of this jeal-

ousy in little children by observing their behavior, for example, at the birth of another
child. Thus a little two-year-old girl, whose
father proudly showed her the newly born
brother—expecting her to feel joy and admiration—merely asked, "When will he die
again?" A mother told me that when she was
feeding her infant at the breast her three-year-
old boy, armed with a stick or some other
pointed object, would come quite close to her,
and she had great difficulty in preventing him
from doing an injury to the baby. This type of
occurrence can be multiplied endlessly. As a
matter of fact, one hears of serious injuries
which children two and three years old inflict
on their younger brothers or sisters if they are
unwisely left alone with them.

We have every reason to regard this jealousy of small children as serious. It springs
from the same motives as the jealousy of
adults, and causes the child the same amount
of suffering as in adult life we endure from
the disturbance of our relation to a beloved
one through unwelcome rivals. The only difference is that the child is more restricted in

his actions than the adult, and thus the satisfaction of his jealous feelings goes no further
than a wish. He wishes the tiresome brothers
and sisters to go away, he would like them to
be dead. To the little child who has not yet
learned to grasp the meaning of death there is,
for the time being, no difference between going away and being dead.

This wish for his brothers' and sisters'
death is thoroughly natural on the part of the
child. The more the child values the possession of the mother, the more violent is this
desire. The child, moreover, is at first completely single-minded in his hostile feelings.
An emotional conflict arises within him only
when he notes that his mother, who loves
these disturbing brothers and sisters (he cannot understand this at all), requires him to
give up these evil desires, share the mother
with them and even love them. Here is the
starting point of all the difficulties in the emotional relations between the brothers and sisters of a family. You probably know from
your own observation of older children how
frequently "family love" represents only the

adult's desire that such a love should exist, and how different the real relationship is from this imaginary one. It is, moreover, a striking proof of the correctness of the situation here described that the jealousy between brothers and sisters is much less when the relations to the mother are not so close. In working-class families, where the mother is able to devote far less care to her children, the loss of tenderness at the birth of younger children is correspondingly less. Hence there is to be found among working-class children much more love and sympathy than in middle-class families. In the latter each child sees in the other children of the family a rival for a very real possession, and accordingly hatred and jealousy, open or hidden, dominate the relations between brothers and sisters.

But this emotional antagonism in which the little child is involved in relation to his brothers and sisters is a comparatively harmless prelude to another and a much more powerful emotional conflict. His brothers and sisters are not the only rivals who compete

with him for the possession of the mother: the
father is far more important. Now the father
plays a twofold part in the little child's life.
The boy hates him as a rival when his father
acts the part of rightful owner of the mother,
when he takes the mother away, goes out with
her, treats her as his property, and insists upon
sleeping with her by himself. But in all other
respects the child loves and admires his father,
relies on his help, believes in his strength and
omnipotence and has no greater desire than
to be like him in the future. Thus there arises
in the boy the extraordinary problem, at first
quite insoluble, that he loves and admires a
person and at the same time hates him and
wishes him dead. In the relation to his brothers and sisters it was only a question of restraining his evil desires in order to please his
mother. Here for the first time one emotion is
in conflict with another emotion. I leave it to
you to imagine for yourselves the further difficulties into which the little boy is plunged
through this conflict: agony at the strength of
his evil wishes, fear of his father's revenge and
the loss of his love, the destruction of all ease

and peace in his relations with his mother, his bad conscience and his mortal dread of death. I shall have more to say about this in another place.

Probably you feel that it would be very interesting to pursue this path of the little child's emotional development, but you do not see how this is related to your own particular work. The children with whom you have to deal are much older and have long got beyond the stage of complete dependence on the mother, the early jealousy, and all the conflicts of the first years of life that I have just described. But you are mistaken. What you discover in the Hort or in the school are just the resultant phenomena of this earlier period of life. The children whom you designate as quarrelsome, asocial, and never contented with anything, are putting their school companions in the place of their brothers and sisters, and there, at school, are fighting out with them the conflicts which they were not able to finish in their own homes. And the older ones who react so violently if you endeavor to exercise the slightest show of authority, or those who are so cowed that they do not even venture to look you in the face or to raise their voices in class, are in truth the same little children, but they have transferred to you the longing for the father's death and the difficult suppression of such wishes, with the resultant anguish and surrender. You get here the explanation of a phenomenon which at first astonished you. It is a fact that the six-year-old children bring with them their ready-made reactions, and that they only repeat them with you. What you see being enacted before your eyes are really additions to and repetitions of very old conflicts but slightly influenced by yourself.

I anticipate a second objection from you. You probably find that the family such as I have depicted to you does not exist at all, at least not in the case of most of the children with whom you have to deal. You very rarely find a mother who bestows on her children such loving care and tenderness and distributes it so impartially. Nor do you often know of a father who lives with his wife on such friendly terms and is at the same time qualified to be the object of the love and admiration of his little son. The picture is as a rule quite different.

But I had a quite definite object in describing to you this model family. I wanted to put before you the difficult position of the child, with his conflicting emotions, even when his external environment is regarded as favorable. Where external conditions are worse and the family life more miserable, the conflict that is going on within the child is still more severe.

Let us assume that the child is not brought up by his own mother, but during this most important first year of his life is put out to nurse, first at one place, then at another, or is taken care of in a home by more or less indifferent nurses who are constantly changing. Ought we not to assume that the lack of this first natural emotional bond will have great influence on the whole of his later life? Or let us take it that the father whom the boy regards as his example and in whose footsteps he seeks to follow is a drunkard, or insane, or a criminal. Then the effort to become like the father, which normally is one of the greatest helps in education, leads in this case to the direct ruin of the child. When the parents are separated and each parent tries to win over the child to his or her side and to represent the other as the guilty party, then the entire emotional development of the child suffers. His confidence is shattered by his critical powers being too early awakened. I will quote to you here the judgment of an eight-year-old boy who made vain efforts to bring his parents together again. He said: "If my father does not love my mother, then my mother does not love my father, then they can't like me. Then I don't want them. And then the whole family is no good." The consequences which such a child deduces from the position of affairs are generally serious. He acts like an employee in a bankrupt firm who has lost all confidence in his principals and no longer therefore feels any pleasure in his work. Thus the child in such circumstances stops work—that is, his normal development is checked and he reacts to the abnormal conditions in some abnormal way.

Here I conclude my lecture. I have laid upon you the difficult task of regarding the incidents which take place in the first years of childhood in the way in which they can be reconstructed by the psychoanalytic method. I do not know how far the details appear to you worthy of belief or improbable. In any case, these discoveries of psychoanalysis have helped to direct the attention of people in general to the significance of the events in the earliest years of childhood. In conclusion, the case of which I am now going to give you details will show you the practical results of such theoretical considerations.

A little while ago a German court of law had to pronounce judgment on a divorce case. In the course of the lawsuit the question arose to which of the parents the two-year-old child should be assigned. The lawyer appearing for the husband proved that the wife, on account of a whole series of traits in her character, was not properly qualified to educate the child. To this the wife's lawyer objected that for a child who was only in his second year it was not a question of education at all, but only of just looking after the child. In order to decide the point at issue the opinion of experts was taken as to the time when a child's education might be said to begin. The specialists who were called belonged partly to the psychoanalytic school, partly to the orthodox scientific school. But they unanimously agreed that *the education of a child begins with his first day of life.*

We have every reason to assume that previous to the discoveries of psychoanalysis the experts would have decided otherwise.

LECTURE II

The Infantile Instinct-Life

I do not feel at all sure as to how you have received the statements in my last lecture, but I venture to surmise that the impression left on you was a twofold one. You probably think, on the one hand, that I have informed you of facts already well known to you, with much unnecessary emphasis. You feel, perhaps, that I falsely assume we are still in the stage when teachers judged their pupils as units apart from their families. I forget, you would say, that today even the youngest teacher, when difficulties arise, thinks first of all of the home environment of the child, of the possibility of an unfavorable influence exercised by the parents, and of the position of the child among his brothers and sisters—that is to say, of the effects produced on the child

by being the eldest or youngest child or half-
way down the family. You always try to explain the child's conduct at school by the way
he is treated at home.

You were quite aware of the fact, long before I lectured to you, that the child's character is greatly influenced by experiences in
the home. On the other hand, you feel that I
have placed before you these simple facts with
much exaggeration. You think I have every-
where interpreted the emotions and acts of
little children by analogy with the correspond-
ing manifestations of adults, and that I describe childish behavior in language generally used only for the behavior of adults. Thus
I have converted the ordinary friction of the
child with his brothers and sisters into serious
death-wishes; and the quite innocent and tender relation of the boy to his mother into the
love of a man who desires a woman sexually.

To you it appears quite natural that the
boy in the intimate daily life with his father
gets to realize the latter's superior power, and
submits unwillingly to the paternal command
and the restrictions on his freedom. But as I

see it, a conflict arises between father and son such as Schiller depicts in *Don Carlos*. You had already heard with astonishment the report that psychoanalysis went so far as to compare the emotional situation of the little child with that of King Oedipus of the Greek story who slew his father and possessed his mother. Thus I have simply proved to you by my arguments that the prejudice which you had always until now felt toward psychoanalysis was not unfounded, and I have merely turned this prejudice into a considered opinion on the ground of your own experience. I will not for the moment support with arguments this psychoanalytic viewpoint. I only ask you to suspend judgment for a little while.

Let us once more return to the verdict given by the German law court, with which, as I have pointed out to you, psychoanalysis is in complete agreement. What have we to conceive as "education" from the first day of life? What is there, indeed, to educate in the tiny creature, so like an animal, of whose mental processes we have hitherto known so little? Where here can educational effort find a point of attack? According to the description I have sketched of the inner life of the child and his relations to the people of his environment, one might perhaps think the answer was simple. The task of education in the case of the little child would be to check alike the evil wishes which are directed against his brothers and sisters and his father, and the longings for his mother, and to prevent their materialization.

But on closer consideration this definition of the earliest stage of education appears unsatisfactory and somewhat ridiculous. The little child stands helpless and powerless amid his adult surroundings. We know he can be preserved from destruction only by the kindness of those around him. Every comparison of his strength with that of those near him can only be to his disadvantage. He has, therefore, not the slightest chance of carrying out his dangerous desires. It is true that in the juvenile courts and children's clinics there are cases in which boys have actually played the part of the father toward the mother as completely as was possible, considering their physical development, or in which a little girl has been used by her own father in the sexual relation. But in all such cases it has never been the strength and energy of the child that has effected this abnormal accomplishment of his emotional wishes, but the abnormal desires of the adults who exploit the child's desires toward them for the satisfaction of their own lusts. In actual life it is as a rule far more important to protect the child from the father's anger than the father from the child's hostility.

The question, therefore, of the definition of education for the first year of life is still unsolved, and we know little about its purport. Perhaps we get a new basis for the answer to this question if—again I refer to the legal verdict quoted earlier—we compare the two ideas of child care and child education.

There is no difficulty about a definition of child care. The rearing of the child consists in the fulfillment of the child's bodily needs. The child's guardian satisfies its hunger, keeps it clean—probably this latter is in response to the adult's desire rather than the child's need—sees it is warm and quiet and protects it from the troubles and dangers of life. She gives the child all it needs without requiring anything in return. Education, on the contrary, always wants something from the child.

It would lead me far beyond my own province here if I were to begin to describe to you the innumerable aims claimed for education in the past and in the present. Educators, that is to say those adults who form the environment of the child, always want to make him what suits them, which consequently differs according to the century, position, rank, class, etc., of the adults. But all these varying aims have one feature in common. The universal aim of education is always to make out of the child a grown-up person who shall not be very different from the grown-up world around him. Consequently we have here the starting point for education. It regards as childlike behavior everything in which the child differs from the adult. Our answer, therefore, to the question concerning the earliest form of education must be as follows: education struggles with the nature of the child or—as the grown-up usually calls it—with his naughtiness.

It would be a mistake for me to spare you the recital of the childish naughtinesses on the ground that every teacher and educator knows them from his own observation. The naughtiness that the child reveals in the school only faintly reflects what is within him. A true description of these characteristics could only be obtained from the people who are continually busied with the little child from infancy to the fifth year. When we question such people we hear something like this: the child is frightfully inconsiderate of others and egotistic; he is only concerned with getting his own way and satisfying his own desires; he is quite indifferent as to whether this hurts others or not. He is dirty and odoriferous; he does not mind catching hold of the most disgusting things or even putting them to his mouth. He is quite shameless so far as his own body is concerned and very curious about the things that other people wish to conceal from him. He is greedy and will steal dainties. He is cruel to all living creatures that are weaker than himself and filled with a perfect lust for destroying inanimate objects. He has an abundance of naughty bodily tricks, he sucks his fingers, he bites his nails, he picks his nose and plays with his sexual organs; he does all these things urged by his intense desire for self-fulfillment, and regards the slightest hindrance as intolerable. Parents in describing the children complain chiefly of two things. They have a feeling of hopelessness; scarcely have they broken the child of one bad habit than another takes its place, and they cannot understand where he gets such habits. Certainly not from his parents' example, and they have so carefully kept their own child away from bad children.

You will say that this account of childish attributes is rather an indictment than an objective statement. But adults, in the matter of children's characteristics, have never taken an objective attitude. Education, seen from the child's point of view throughout the centuries, is something like a very severe teacher who comes, full of indignation beforehand, to investigate the affairs of his pupils. He will never succeed in obtaining the real facts of the case and the actual relationship of events if he does not wisely learn to postpone judgment until . the end of his investigation. The "naughtinesses" of children, as the parents call them, are only a chaotic disorderly mass of child-characteristics. There is nothing to be done except to lament them!

But up till now science also has not regarded the child in a mucn more objective light. It has adopted the expedient of denying all those features which did not appear to fit into the picture which, working from quite other hypotheses, it had drawn of the child's nature. It was psychoanalysis that first freed itself from the judgments, the assumptions and the prejudices with which adults have from time immemorial approached this matter of estimating the nature of children. As a result, many bad habits, hitherto quite inexplicable, will be found to arrange themselves into an organic whole in a most surprising way. Instead of arbitrary acts they are discovered to be an inevitable sequence of events in accordance with the stages of development, such as we have long recognized in the development of the physical body. Psychoanalysis found also the answer to the parents' two main complaints about their children. The quick change from one bad habit to another and its formation without any external influence: these things ceased to be puzzling problems when the naughty habits signified no deplorable, haphazard abnormalities of the child, but the natural, normal links in a predetermined chain of development.

The first indication of such an order in the phenomena was the observation that the parts of the body with which the child plays his naughty tricks were not chosen arbitrarily, but were determined in a precise sequence. You will remember, perhaps, that in our first talk we traced the close link between the child and its mother to the first nourishment and care given to the child by the mother. The first naughty behavior of the child arises from the same cause and is connected with the same place.

In the first weeks of his existence food plays the most important part in his life, and at this time his mouth and all connected with it are the most important parts of his body to him. The child finds sucking at his mother's breast and getting the flow of milk with his mouth very pleasant, and the wish for the continuation and repetition of this sensual experience remains with him even when he has satisfied his hunger. He soon learns how to procure this delightful feeling again, independently of the food obtained and the person who suckles him, by sucking his own finger. Then we say the child "sucks." His face as he does this has the same contented expression as when his mother is suckling him, and consequently we are never doubtful concerning the motive of this act of sucking. We see that the child sucks because he enjoys sucking. The pleasure gained from sucking, which was originally only pleasure incidental to the taking of nourishment, has now become a pleasure in itself, and this activity which the child enjoys and the grownups object to is regarded as a naughty habit. At this time the pleasure-giving activity of the mouth is by no means confined to taking food and sucking. The child acts as if he would like to become acquainted with the whole world within his reach by means of his mouth. He bites, he licks and tastes everything near him—characteristics which the grownups around him certainly do not regard as desirable, owing to the difficulty of keeping the child clean, and because of the consequent danger to his health. The pre-eminent part played by the mouth as the source of such pleasurable experience lasts more or less during the whole of the first year of life. When you recall our list of accusations against the child you will find there the naughty habits which have certainly their origin at this period, but which continue into a far later age—I refer to greediness and love of dainties.

But the next bodily zone which now fills the foreground and takes the significant place formerly held by the mouth is determined by external experiences. Up till this time the grown-up world has been very tolerant toward the child, occupying itself, indeed, almost entirely in caring for him, the only exceptions being that he has to become accustomed to habits of order and regularity in taking his food and going to sleep. But now there gradually enters into the child's life a very important factor—training in cleanliness. His mother or his nurse endeavors to break him of the habit of wetting and dirtying himself. It is not easy to teach the child to control these functions. Indeed, one might say that so far as training the child is concerned the whole of the second year of life is given over to very active efforts to inculcate cleanliness.

But you feel that the child ought not to be blamed as naughty because a long time is required to teach him cleanliness. His sphincter muscles may not yet be sufficiently developed to enable him to retain his urine and regulate his movements. That is quite right so far as the earliest period of training in cleanliness is concerned; but later it is otherwise. A closer observation of the child makes one suspect that he is no longer unable to keep himself clean, but that he is merely protecting his right to eject his excreta when it pleases him, and he will certainly not allow anyone to take

from him his right to this product of his own
body. He shows extraordinary interest in his
own feces; he tries to touch them, to play with
them and, indeed, if he is not prevented at the
right moment, even to put them into his
mouth. We can easily explain, by the expression on his face and the ardor which he shows
while doing it, the motive for his activity. It
gives the child obvious delight, it is pleasurable. But this pleasure has nothing now to do
with the strength or weakness of the sphincter
muscle of the bladder or the anus. Just as the
infant, in taking his food from his mother's
breast, discovered as an additional gain a pleasure in everything connected with the mouth,
so in the same way he experiences as an incidental advantage a pleasure in his anus after
his bowels have acted. The area round his
anus becomes at this time the most important
part of his body. Just as in the period of being
suckled the child always sought to procure for
himself the pleasure his mouth gave him, independently of food, so he now tries by with-
holding his feces and playing about with that
part of his body to get the same pleasure. And

if his training actively prevents his doing this he still clings, in the more legitimate games with sand, water and mud and later in his daubing about with paints, to the memory of the pleasure he once prized so greatly.

Adults have always complained that at this period the child is dirty and has horrid habits. At the same time they were always inclined to excuse the child. He was still so little and stupid, his aesthetic sense was not yet sufficiently cultivated for him to understand rightly the difference between clean and dirty, or his sense of smell had not been exercised enough to distinguish between a sweet smell and an offensive smell.

I am of the opinion that the observers of children are to some extent laboring here under an error of judgment. Whoever has carefully observed a small child of somewhere about two years of age must have noticed that he distinguishes with extraordinary exactitude between the different smells. His difference from the adults lies in his different appraisal of the various smells. The scent of any particular flower which delights an adult will leave the child quite indifferent unless the former has been accustomed to say, "Oh, how lovely!" when smelling the flower. But what smells horrid to us smells good to the child. Of course, we can, if we like, consider the child naughty because nasty smells give him pleasure!

We find a repetition of this relation to adult appraisals in other childlike peculiarities. For centuries the cruelty of children has been noted without any explanation being given except childish folly. When a child tears off the legs and wings of butterflies and flies, kills or tortures birds or vents his rage for destruction on his playthings or articles in daily use, his elders excuse it on the ground of lack of capacity to feel for a different living creature, or his slight comprehension of the money value of things. But our observation teaches us something different. We hold that the child tortures animals, not because he does not understand that it adds to their suffering, but just because he wants to add to their sufferings, and small, defenseless beetles are the least dangerous of creatures. The child destroys objects because the actual value of such things, compared with the joy he experiences in their destruction, does not come into consideration at all. But we can guess at the motive of his act, just as we did when he sucked his thumb and played with dirty things, from the expression of his face and the wild joy with which he pursues his purpose. Here again he acts thus because it gives him pleasure.

After the training in cleanliness has completely attained its end, and the child, in spite of his opposition, has been taught how to control his movements, the part round his anus loses its importance as a means of acquiring pleasurable sensations. Instead, another part of his body emerges as still more important. The child begins to play with his genitals. At this time his thirst for knowledge is directed toward the discovery of the differences between his own body and those of his brothers and sisters and playfellows. He delights in showing his sexual parts naked to other children, and in return demands to see theirs. His passion for asking questions, of which his

elders complain, has as its basis these problems—the difference between the sexes and its
connection with the origin of children, which
he somehow or other dimly feels. But the culminating point of the development which the
child reaches just at this time in many directions, that is, in his fourth or fifth year, seems
to the adults who are training him the culminating point in his undesirable habits.

We know that the child acts throughout
the whole period of development above described as if there were nothing more important than the gratifying of his own pleasures
and the fulfilling of his powerful instincts,
whereas education proceeds as if the preven-
tion of these objects was its most important
task. In consequence there arises a kind of
"guerilla war" between educator and child.
Education wants to substitute for love of dirt
a disgust of dirt, for shamelessness a feeling of
shame, for cruelty sympathy, and in place of a
rage for destructiveness a desire to cherish
things. Curiosity and the desire to handle
one's own body must be eliminated by prohibitions, lack of consideration for others

must be replaced by consideration, egotism by altruism. Step by step education aims at the exact opposite of the child's instinctive desires.

As we have seen, to the child the attainment of pleasure is the main object of life. The adult wants to teach him to regard the claims of the external world as more important than these instinctive urges. The child is impatient, he cannot endure any delay and acts only for the moment; the grown-up person teaches him to postpone the gratification of his impulses and to take heed of the future.

It will have struck you that my description has not made any essential distinction between the pleasure gained by sucking and by playing with the genitals, that is, masturbation. As a matter of fact, from the standpoint of psychoanalysis no such distinction exists. All the pleasurable acts which have been described here are efforts toward the satisfaction of instinctive impulses. Psychoanalysis invests them all with sexual significance, whether they are concerned with the actual sexual organs, or the mouth, or the anus. The role which the genitals play in the fourth or fifth year of the child's life is exactly that of the mouth in the first year or the anus in the second year. The genital zone appears to us only in retrospect as so significant when we regard it from the standpoint of adult sexual life, in which the genitals are the specific organs of that sexual life. But, even so, the genital zones in early childhood do possess a certain significance. The sensual pleasure derived from them serves as a preparation for and an introduction to the sexual act proper.

The fact that the bodily regions from which the little child gains his first sensual pleasures play a part, though a subordinate one, in the sexual life of the adult, does not seem to you perhaps a sufficient reason for designating these regions of the child's pleasure-seeking activity as sexual in the same sense as the direct genital activity. But psychoanalysis justifies this classification on account of still another circumstance. There are abnormal cases in which one or other of these infantile impulses retains its primacy, refusing to transfer itself to the specific genital zone, and maintains this primacy in adult life. It disputes the part played by the genital regions and regards the attainment of sexual pleasure as bound up with itself alone. Such beings are designated as perverts. It is characteristic of them that in a very important aspect of their life, namely, in their sexuality, they remain at the stage of the little child, or possibly, at some time or another, have returned to that stage.

Now the understanding of this abnormality in adult sexual life makes it possible for us, perhaps for the first time, to understand why education is so very zealous in restraining the child from the gratification of his impulses. The phases of development which the child has to go through are simply stages on the way to a quite definitely prescribed goal. When one of these stopping-places appears too attractive there is the danger that the child begins to settle down there permanently and refuses to continue the journey or to advance to a further stage of development. Long before there was any scientific proof of this conception educators in all ages acted as if they recognized these dangers. Consequently, they re-

garded it as their task to get the child through
his phases of development without his ever at-
taining any real satisfaction and pleasure
from any one stage except the last.

The means which from time immemorial
education has adopted in its struggle to prevent the child from obtaining this dreaded
sensual gratification are of two kinds. It may
be the child is warned: If you suck your
thumb any more it will be cut off, a threat
which nurses and picture books (take, for example, *Slovenly Peter*) are accustomed to repeat on all occasions and with every kind of
variation. They try to frighten the child by
the idea of actual violence and injury to a necessary and much-prized part of his body, and
to make him renounce this kind of pleasure.
Or it may be people say: If you do that I cannot love you any more! Here he is brought
face to face with the possibility of the loss of
his parents' love. Both threats operate, owing
to the situation of the child as we have already
learned to understand it in the last lecture—
that is, his complete helplessness and power-
lessness in the midst of an overwhelming

adult world, and his exclusive dependence upon his parents' love.

Both methods are usually equally effective. Under the pressure of such appalling dangers the child, indeed, learns to abandon his primitive designs. At first when he discontinues these practices he merely pretends, from fear of grownups or from love of them, that he has changed his attitude. He begins to designate as horrid what seems to him lovely, and as delightful and pleasurable what is displeasing to him. As he assimilates more and more the adults' standpoint he accepts their values as the true ones. He now begins to forget that he has ever felt otherwise, and gradually denies all that he had desired in his earlier days and prevents a return to his earlier enjoyment by an absolute reversal of the feelings connected with the former sensual satisfaction. The more complete this transference, the more contented are the grownups with their educational efforts.

This renunciation of the pleasure derived from his infantile impulses which is forced upon the child has two important effects on his mental development. He now pitilessly applies this standard which has been forced upon himself to the rest of the world. He becomes throughout his life intolerant toward those who have not achieved the same development as himself and still allow themselves the sensual gratification from one or other of these earlier sources. The moral indignation which is aroused by such acts is the measure of the effort he himself has had to make to conquer his instinctive impulses.

Coincident with the rejection by his memory of the pleasurable experiences once so dearly prized, he also pushes from his recollection that whole period of his life, with all the feelings and experiences which belong to it. He forgets his past, which now in retrospect can appear to him only as unworthy and repulsive. But it is just because of this that he has that gap in his memory, that impenetrable barrier and that inaccessibility with regard to the first most important experiences of childhood which so greatly astonished us at the last lecture.

LECTURE III

The Latency Period

I have now during two lectures kept you far removed from the sphere of your own particular interests. I have engaged your attention for the emotional condition and the development of the instincts of the tiny child—a subject, indeed, which you most likely think could only have practical significance for mothers, nurses and, at the most, for the kindergarten teachers. I should not like you to think, on account of my choice of material, that I underestimate the problems which arise in your work with older children. But my object was to bring before you in the course of these lectures many of the fundamental ideas of psychoanalysis, and, in order to develop them vividly for you, I required some very definite material which only the first years of childhood can supply.

Let us examine what you have already learned from the things you have now heard concerning the theory of psychoanalysis, in order that I may ultimately justify the roundabout ways into which I have led you. From the very beginning I asserted that human beings are acquainted with only a fragment of their own inner life, and know nothing about a great many of the feelings and thoughts which go on within them—that is to say, that all these things happen unconsciously, without their awareness. You might reply that therefore we ought to be modest. In the vast mass of stimuli pressing upon man from within and without, which he receives and elaborates, it is not at all possible to retain everything in consciousness, it should suffice if one knows the most important things. But the example of the big gap in memory in which the childhood years are hidden must shake this conception. We have seen that the importance of any event is by no means a guarantee of its permanence in our memory; indeed, on the contrary, it is just the most significant impressions that regularly escape recollection. At the same time experience shows that this forgotten part of the inner world has the curious characteristic of retaining its dynamic force when it disappears from memory. It exercises a decisive influence on the child's life, shapes his relations to the people around him and reveals itself in his daily conduct. This twofold characteristic of the experiences of childhood, so contrary to all your expectations, its disappearance into the void while retaining all its power to influence, has given you a good idea of the conception of the *unconscious* in psychoanalysis.

You have, in addition, learned how the forgetting of important impressions may arise. The child would probably be inclined to remember clearly his first very highly valued desires and the satisfaction of the impulses so dearly treasured. He responds to an external pressure when he turns away from them, pushes them aside with a great expenditure of energy and refuses to know anything more about them. We say, then, that he has *repressed* them.

You have further realized that education

has not yet accepted the fact of the child's accomplishment of this act of repression. It obviously fears that the characteristics pushed on one side with so much difficulty might at a favorable opportunity emerge again from the depths. It is, therefore, not content to break the child of a habit which it regards as bad, but it strives to put every obstacle in the way of its re-emergence. Thus there arises the reversal of the original feelings and characteristics in the manner I have already described to you.

Let us assume that a little child of about two years has the desire to put his excreta in his mouth. He learns through the pressure of education not only to reject such an action which he now knows as dirty and to renounce his original desire, but also to feel disgust for it. He gets now a feeling of nausea in connection with his excrement and a desire to vomit, obviously the answer to the original wish to put something into his mouth. To use his mouth for such an action becomes quite impossible for him owing to this feeling of repulsion. Psychoanalysis calls such a later acquired attribute, which has arisen from a conflict and as a reaction against an infantile impulse, a *reaction-formation.* When later on we discover in a child an unusually strong sense of sympathy, an unusual modesty or a feeling of nausea which is easily aroused, we may conclude that in his earliest years he had been specially cruel, shameless, or dirty in his habits. It is essential that this reaction should be strong in order to prevent a relapse into his earlier habits.

But this reversal to the exact opposite in the shape of a reaction-formation is only one of the ways in which the child can discard an attribute. Another way is to transform an undesirable activity into a more desirable one. I have already given you an example of this kind. The little child who has enjoyed playing about with his own excreta need not completely forego this pleasure in order to escape blame from his teacher. He can seek a substitute for this pleasure, finding, for example, in games with sand and water a substitute for his preoccupation with urine and feces, and, according to the opportunities given him, he builds things in a sand heap or digs in the garden or makes canals, just as little girls learn to wash their dolls' clothes.

The pleasure in smearing things is, as we have already indicated, continued in the use of paints and colored chalks. In each of these social and often useful activities, thoroughly approved by adults, the child enjoys some portion of the pleasure originally experienced. To this refinement of an impulse, and its diversion to an aim estimated by education as of higher value, psychoanalysis has given the name of *sublimation*.

You have, however, been able to gather from the two previous lectures something more than merely the definition of some of the fundamental ideas of psychoanalysis. You have learned that there are ideas and idea-complexes which, through their becoming definitely associated together, play a dominant role in the emotional life of the child. They dominate certain years of life, then they are repressed and are no longer to be discovered in the consciousness of the adult without further investigation. The relation of the little child to his parents is an example of such an association of ideas. Psychoanalysis, as you have already heard, discovers bchind this relationship the same motives and desires which inspired the deeds of King Oedipus, and has given the name of the *Oedipus complex* to it. Another such complex of ideas is to be seen in the effect of the threats which education employs to make the child submit to its wishes. As the purport of these threats—even if they are only hinted at—is to cut off an important part of the child's body—his hand, or tongue, or his penis—psychoanalysis has named this complex the *castration complex*.

Furthermore, in my first talk, you became acquainted with the fact that the way in which the child experiences these earliest complexes, especially his relations to his parents, becomes the pattern for all his later experiences. There is in him a compulsion to repeat in later life the pattern of his earlier love and hate, rebellion and submission, disloyalty and loyalty. It is not a matter of indifference for the child's later life that he has an inward urge to choose his love-relations, his friends and even his professional career so that he obtains almost a repetition of his repressed childhood's experiences. We say, as you saw in the example of the relation of the school child to his teachers, that the child *transfers* his emotional attitude toward an earlier figure on to a person in the present. It is obvious that the child must very often reinterpret or misunderstand the real, actual situation, and has to distort it in all sorts of ways in order to make such an emotional transference at all possible.

Finally, you found in my description of the childish instinctual development a confirmation of the assertion so often heard that psychoanalysis extends the conception of the sexual beyond the hitherto customary limits. It designates as sexual a series of childish activities which had formerly been regarded as completely harmless and far removed from anything sexual. Psychoanalysis, in opposition to all the teaching you have ever known, asserts that the sexual instincts of man do not suddenly awaken between the thirteenth and fifteenth year, i.e. at puberty, but operate from the outset of the child's development, change gradually from one form to another, progress from one stage to another, until at last adult sexual life is achieved as the final result of this long series of developments. The energy with which the sexual instincts function in all these phases is in its nature always the same, and only different in degree at different periods.

Psychoanalysis calls this sexual energy *libido*. The theory of the development of the childish impulses is the most important part of the new psychoanalytic science, and at the same time it is this theory that from the outset has made enemies for psychoanalysis. Very likely this has been the reason why so many of you have hitherto held yourselves scrupulously aloof from analytic theories.

I think you may be content with this summary of the theoretical knowledge which you have hitherto possessed of psychoanalysis. You have become acquainted with a number of the most important fundamental ideas of psychoanalysis and with its customary terminology. You have met with the idea of the *unconscious, repression, reaction-formation, sublimation, transference,* the *Oedipus com-*

plex and the *castration complex*, the *libido* and the theory of *infantile sexuality*. Perhaps these conceptions, but recently worked out, will help us very much in our further task, that of investigating the next period in the child's life.

We will now continue the account of the child from the point where we left off in our last discussion. This was at his fifth or sixth year, at that period when the child is entrusted to the public educational institutions and consequently claims all your interest.

Let us, in the light of the knowledge we have now acquired, examine the complaint made by teachers in the kindergarten and the school that the little children come to them as already finished human beings. We can now fully confirm the teachers in the accuracy of this impression, from our own knowledge of the inner situation of the child. The little child, by the time he comes to the school or kindergarten for the first time, has already had a host of profound emotional experiences. He has suffered a curtailment of his original egoism through love of a particular person; he has experienced a violent desire for the possession of this beloved person; and he has defended his rights by death-wishes directed against others and by outbreaks of jealousy. In his relation to his father he has become acquainted with feelings of respect and admiration, tormenting feelings of competition with a stronger rival, the feeling of impotence and the depressing effect of a disappointment in love. He has, moreover, already passed through a complicated instinct-development and has learned how hard it is to be obliged to confront conflicting forces in his own personality.

Under the pressure of education he has suffered terrible fears and anxiety, and accomplished enormous changes within himself. Burdened with this past, the child is indeed anything but a blank sheet. The transformation which has taken place within him is verily amazing. Out of the creature so like an animal, so dependent on others, and to those around him almost intolerable, a more or less reasonable human being has been evolved. The school child who enters the classroom is consequently prepared to find that he is there only one among many, and from this time onward he cannot count on any privileged position. He has learned something of social adaptation. Instead of continually seeking to gratify his desires, as formerly, he is now prepared to do what is required of him and to confine his pleasures to the times allowed for them. His interest in seeing everything and finding out the intimate mysteries of his environment has now been transformed into a thirst for knowledge and a love of learning. In place of the revelations and explanations which he longed for earlier he is now prepared to obtain a knowledge of letters and numbers.

Those of you who are workers at the Infant Horts will probably think that I am describing the good behavior of the child in too glowing colors, just as in my last talk with you I painted his naughtiness too black. You feel you have not met such good children. But you must not forget that the Children's Horts, as they are conducted today, only receive cases in which the earliest education of the chil-

dren, owing to some internal or external circumstances, has not been entirely satisfactory.
On the other hand, the teachers in the ordinary schools will recognize many of their pupils in my description and will not accuse me
of exaggeration.

This might be, indeed, a splendid proof of
the practical possibilities and the enormous
influence of education. The parents to whom,
speaking generally, must be ascribed the
credit for the earliest education, have every
right to be somewhat proud if they have succeeded in making out of the crying, trouble-
some, and dirty infant a well-behaved school
child. There are not many spheres in this
world where similar transformations are accomplished.

But we should still more unreservedly ad-
mire the work which the parents have per-
formed if two considerations were not forced
upon us in judging its results. One of these
considerations arises from observation. Whoever has had the opportunity of being much
with three-to-four-year-old children, or of
playing with them, is amazed at the wealth of

their fantasy, the extent of their vision, the
lucidity of their minds and the inflexible logic
of their questions and conclusions. Yet the
very same children, when of school age, appear to the adult in close contact with them
rather silly, superficial, and somewhat unin-
teresting. We ask with astonishment whatever
has become of the child's shrewdness and originality! Psychoanalysis reveals to us that these
gifts of the little child have not been able to
hold their own against the demands which
have been made upon him; after the expiration of his fifth year they are as good as
vanished. Obviously, to bring up "good" children is not without its dangers. The repres-
sions which are required to achieve this result,
the reaction-formations and the sublimations
which have to be built up, are paid for at a
quite definite cost. The originality of the
child, together with a great deal of his energy
and his talents, are sacrificed to being "good."
If the older children, compared with the little
child, strike us as dull and inactive the impression is absolutely correct. The limitations
which are placed upon their thinking, and the

obstacles put in the way of their original activities, result in dullness and incapacity to act.

But if in this connection parents have little cause to be very proud of their success, in another direction likewise it is somewhat doubtful if they deserve much credit. That is to say, we have no guarantee at all whether the good behavior of the older child is the product of education or simply the consequence of having reached a certain period of development. We have still no essential data whereby to decide what would happen if little children were allowed to develop by themselves. We do not know whether they would grow up like little savages or whether, without any external help, they would pass through a series of modifications. It is quite certain that education influences the child tremendously in various directions, but the question remains unanswered as to what would happen if the adults round a child refrained from interfering with him in any way.

An important experiment to elucidate this problem was made from the psychoanalytic standpoint, but unfortunately it was not completed. The Russian analyst, Mme. Vera Schmidt, founded in Moscow in 1921 a children's home for thirty children from one to five years old. The name, the Children's Home Laboratory, which she gave to it characterized this institute as a kind of scientific experimental station. Mme. Schmidt's object was to surround this little group of children with scientifically trained teachers employed to observe quietly the various emotional and instinctual manifestations of the children; and, though the teachers would help and stimulate, they were to interfere as little as possible with the changes that were taking place in the children. By such means it would gradually be established whether the various phases which follow one another in the child's first years arise spontaneously and then disappear without any direct educational influence, and also whether the child, without being forced, would abandon his pleasure-activities and the sources of pleasure after a certain period and exchange them for new ones.

Mme. Vera Schmidt's Children's Home

Laboratory, on account of external difficulties, was not long enough established to complete this new kind of educational experiment, except in the case of one child. The question, therefore, of how much credit for the changes in the child is to be ascribed exclusively to the earliest education remains unsolved until it becomes possible to undertake again a similar experiment under more favorable circumstances.

But whether this phenomenon is to be ascribed to the training of the parents or simply to be regarded as the necessary characteristic of that particular stage of life, observation in any case teaches us that in the fifth or sixth year the overwhelming force of the infantile instinct slowly dies down. The culminating point in the child's violent emotional manifestations and insistent instinctual desires has already been passed by his fourth or fifth year, and the child gradually arrives at a kind of peace. It appears as if he had taken a great leap to become completely grown-up, just as the animal develops from birth to maturity without a break, and thereby cuts off all possibility

of change. But with the child the case is otherwise. In his fifth or sixth year he suddenly
comes to a standstill in his instinctual development without, however, having brought it
to any definite conclusion. He loses the interest in the gratification of his instincts which so
surprised us at first in the little child. He now
for the first time begins to be like the picture
of the "good" child which until now has only
existed in the wish-fantasy of the grownups.

But the instincts which had hitherto caused
the child to seek satisfaction in all kinds of
ways have not ceased to exist; they are only
less noticeable outwardly. They are latent,
dormant, and only to awaken again after a
period of years with renewed vigor. Adolescence, which has so long been regarded as the
period when sexual feeling has its beginning,
is thus merely a second edition of a development now indeed completed, but which began at birth and came to a standstill at the end
of the first period of childhood. If we follow
the growth of a child from this first period of
childhood, through this quiet time—the
latency period as it is named in psychoanalysis

—to the stage of puberty, we shall find that the child once more experiences, in a new edition, all the old difficulties which had lain dormant. The emotional situation which had caused him special conflicts as a little child, such as the rivalry with his father or the peculiarly difficult repression of a forbidden pleasure (the love of dirt, perhaps), will burst forth again, creating extraordinary difficulty. Thus the earliest period of the child's life often shows, even in the minutest details, far-reaching similarities with the period of adolescence. And yet in the calmer latency period the child resembles in many respects a sensible, sedate adult.

Here again, from time immemorial, education has acted as if it had been guided by a good psychological understanding of the child's inner situation. It utilizes the latency period, in which the child is no longer exclusively engrossed with his inner conflicts and is less disturbed by his instincts, to begin the training of his intellect. Teachers in the schools have from the beginning of time be-

haved as if they understood that the child at
this period is the more capable of learning the
less subject he is to his instincts, and consequently they have punished most severely and
pursued pitilessly the child at school who
makes manifest his instinctual desires or seeks
pleasure satisfaction.

Here the tasks of the school and the Hort
diverge. The object of the school is above all
else instruction—that is to say, the development of the mind, the imparting of new ideas
and of knowledge and the arousing of mental
capacity. The training in the Children's Hort,
on the contrary, has the task of supplement-
ing that training of the impulses which has
probably not been completed in the child's
infancy. The educators there know they have
only a limited time at their disposal; they
know that the sexual instinct, which bursts
forth anew in puberty and overwhelms the
child with its force, marks also the end of his
educability. The success or failure of this later
education in many cases determines whether
it is possible at this later period to establish

from the outside a reasonable agreement between the child's ego, the urge of his impulses, and the demands of society.

You will want to know finally how the possibilities of education in infancy and in the latency period stand in relation to one another. Is there a difference between the attitude of the little child to his parents and that of the older child to his teachers and tutors? Does the teacher simply inherit the role of the parents, and must he play the part of the father and mother, and, as they do, work with threats of castration, fear of the loss of love and manifestations of tenderness? When we think of the difficulties which the child has to endure at the height of his Oedipus complex we are right to be alarmed at the idea of similar conflicts, many times multiplied, to be suffered in the intercourse between the class and its teacher. It is not possible to imagine a teacher playing the part of a mother successfully in a large Children's Hort, and doing justice to the claims of each individual child without arousing outbreaks of jealousy on all sides. It must be equally difficult for the teacher, as father of so many, to remain continually the object of fear, the goal of all these insurgent tendencies, and yet at the same time the personal friend of each.

But we forget that the child's emotional situation also has in the meantime altered; his relations to his parents no longer assume the old form. As the childish instincts begin to weaken at this stage of life, the passionate feelings which have hitherto dominated the relation of the child to his father and mother also weaken. Here again we cannot say if this change simply corresponds to a new phase of development upon which the child enters at this age, or whether the child's passionate love-demands gradually succumb to the many unavoidable disillusionments and privations caused by the parents. In any case, the relation between the child and his parents becomes calmer, less passionate, and loses its exclusiveness. The child begins to see his parents in a more reasonable light, to correct his over-estimate of his father, whom up to now he has regarded as omnipotent, and to see things in their true perspective. The love of his mother, which in his earliest childhood is almost adult love, passionately desirous and insatiable, now gives place to a tenderness which makes fewer claims and is more critical. At the same time the child tries to get a certain amount of freedom from his parents, and seeks independently of them new objects for his love and admiration. A process of detachment now begins which continues throughout the whole of the latency period. It is a sign of satisfactory development if, on the termination of puberty, the dependence on the beloved beings of childhood's days has come to an end. The sexual instinct at this period, after having come successfully through all the intervening phases, now reaches the adult genital stage, and should be combined with the love of another who does not belong to his own family.

But this detachment of the child from the earliest and most important of his love objects only succeeds on one very definite condition. It is as if the parents said: You can certainly go away, but you must take us with you. That is to say, the influence of the parents does not end with removal from them and not even with the abatement of feeling for them. Their influence simply changes from a direct to an indirect one. We know that the little child obeys his father's or mother's orders only when he is in their immediate environment and has to fear a direct reprimand from them or their personal interference. Left alone, he follows without scruple his own wishes. But after his second or third year his behavior alters. He is now well aware, even when the person in authority has left the room, of what is permitted and what forbidden, and can regulate his actions accordingly. We say that besides the forces that influence him from without he has also developed an inner force which determines his behavior.

Among psychoanalysts there exists no doubt as to the origin of this inner voice, or conscience, as it is generally designated. It is the continuation of the voice of the parents which is now operative from within instead of, as formerly, from without. The child has absorbed, as it were, a part of his father or mother, or rather the orders and prohibitions which he has constantly received from them, and made these an essential part of his being. In the course of growth this intensified parental part of him assumes ever more and more the role of the parents in the material world, demanding and forbidding certain things. It now continues from within the education of the child who has already become independent of his actual parents. The child gives to this part of his being which has come originally from without a very special place of honor in his own ego, regards it as an ideal, and is prepared to submit to it, often indeed more slavishly, than in his younger days he had submitted to his actual parents.

The poor ego of the child must henceforth strive to fulfill the demands of this ideal—the *superego,* as psychoanalysis names it. When the child does not obey it, he begins to "feel" his dissatisfaction as "inner dissatisfaction," and the sense of satisfaction when he acts in accordance with the will of this superego as "inner satisfaction." Thus the old relation between the child and the parents continues within the child, and the severity or mildness with which the parents have treated the child is reflected in the attitude of the superego to the ego.

Here, looking backward, we can say: The price which the child has to pay for detaching himself from his parents is their incorporation in his own personality. The success of this incorporation is at the same time also the measure of the permanent success of education.

Our question concerning the differences between the possibility of education in the earliest period of childhood and in the latency period is now no longer difficult to answer.

The earliest educators and the little child are opposed to each other like two hostile factions. The parents want something that the child does not want; the child wants what the parents do not want. The child pursues his aims with a wholly undivided passion; nothing remains to the parents but threats and the employment of force. Here one point of view is diametrically opposed to the other. The fact that the victory is nearly always won by the parents is only to be ascribed to their superior physical strength.

The situation is quite otherwise in the latency period. The child that now confronts the educator is no longer an undivided simple being. He is, as we have learned, divided within himself. Even if his ego occasionally still pursues its earlier aims, his superego, the successor to his parents, is on the side of the educators. It is now that the wisdom of the adults determines the extent of educational possibilities. The educator acts mistakenly when he treats the child as if the latter were still his absolute enemy, and by so doing he deprives himself of a great advantage. He merely requires to recognize the cleavage that has arisen in the child and to adapt himself to it. If he succeeds in winning the superego to his side and allying with it then two are working against one. He will have no more trouble in influencing the child in any way he wishes.

Our question regarding the relations between the teacher and the class or group is now also easier to answer. We see from what has already been said that the teacher inherits more than merely the child's Oedipus complex. As long as the teacher has the guidance of a group of children under his control he assumes for each one of them the role of his superego, and in this way acquires the right to the child's submission. If he were just the father of each child, then all the unsolved conflicts of early childhood would take place around him, and moreover his group would be torn asunder by jealousies. If he does succeed in becoming the universal superego, the ideal of all, then compulsory submission changes into voluntary submission, and the children of his group are combined under him into one united whole.

LECTURE IV

The Relation Between
Psychoanalysis and Pedagogy

We must not demand too much from one another. You must not expect that in four short lectures I shall succeed in presenting to you more than the most important principles of a science the study of which would require many years. I, on the other hand, cannot expect you to remember all the details which I have put before you. Out of my summary, condensed from a great abundance of data and thereby probably often confusing, perhaps you will be able to retain for your guidance only three of the characteristic viewpoints of psychoanalysis.

The first of these ideas is concerned with the division of time. Psychoanalysis distinguishes, as you have already learned, three different periods in the life of the child: early childhood up to about the end of the fifth year; the latency period to the beginning of the prepuberty stage, about the eleventh, twelfth, or thirteenth year; and puberty, which leads into adult life. In each period there is a different emotional reaction of the child to those around him, and a different stage of instinctual development, each of which is normal and characteristic. A special attribute of the child, or his method of reaction, cannot therefore be judged without reference to the specific period of his life. An act of instinctive cruelty or shamelessness, for example, which belongs to the early period and to puberty, will cause anxiety to the observer if it occurs in the latency period, and if found in adult life will have, perhaps, to be judged as a perversity. The strong link with the parents, which is natural and desirable in the first period and in the latency period, is a sign of retarded development if it still exists at the end of puberty. The strong urge to rebel and to have inner freedom which in puberty facilitates the emergence into normal adult life may be regarded as an obstacle to the right development of the ego in earliest childhood or in the latency period.

The second aspect is connected with the inner growth of the childish personality. You have probably up till now pictured to yourself the child with whom you have to deal as a homogeneous being, and consequently have not been able to explain the difference between what he wants to do and what he is able to do, the clash between his intentions and his actions. The psychoanalytic conception shows you the personality of the child as of a threefold nature, consisting of the instinctual life, the ego, and the superego, which is derived from the relationship with his parents. The contradictions in his behavior are to be explained, therefore, when you learn to recognize behind his different reactions that part of his being which at this particular moment predominates.

The third principle is concerned with the interaction between these divisions of the childish personality; we must not imagine this to be a peaceful process, but rather a con-

flict. The issue of such a duel, for example, between the ego of the child and an instinctive
wish he knows to be undesirable, depends
upon the relative strength of the libido at the
disposal of the instinctive impulses compared
with the energy of the repressing force derived from the superego.

But I fear, indeed, that these three principles for practical application which I have put
briefly before you do not give you all that you
hoped to get from psychoanalysis in the way
of help for your work. Probably you seek practical advice which will be a guidance to you
rather than an extension of your theoretical
knowledge. You want to know for certain
which methods of education are the most to be
recommended; which must be absolutely
avoided if you do not want to imperil the
child's whole development. Above all, you
want to know whether we shall continue with
more education, or give less than we have in
the past.

In answer to the last question it should be
said that psychoanalysis, whenever it has come
into contact with pedagogy, has always ex-

pressed the wish to limit education. Psychoanalysis has brought before us the quite
definite danger arising from education. You
have learned how the child is forced to fulfill
the demands of the adult world around him.
You know that he conquers his first great emotional attachments by identification with the
beloved and feared adults. He escapes from
their external influence, but meanwhile es-
tablishes a court of judgment within, mod-
eled on the authority of those beings, which
continues to maintain this influence within
him. This incorporation of the parent-figures
is the dangerous step. When this takes place
the prohibitions and demands become fixed
and unchangeable. In place of living beings
they become an historical background which
is incapable of adapting itself to progressive
external changes. In reality the parent-figures
would be influenced by reason in their conduct and would be accessible to the claims of
a new situation. Naturally they would be prepared to concede to the thirty-year-old man
what was forbidden to the three-year-old
child. But that part of the ego which has been

formed from the demands and standards of the parents remains inexorable.

The following examples are given to elucidate these points. I know a boy who was extremely fond of dainties in his earliest years. As his passion for dainties was too great to be satisfied by legitimate means, he hit upon all kinds of unlawful expedients and dodges in order to procure sweets, spent all the money he possessed upon them and was not too particular as to how he procured more. Education was called upon to act; the boy was forbidden sweets, and his passionate devotion to his mother, who had interfered with his pleasure, gave special emphasis to the prohibition. His extreme fondness for dainties disappeared, to the great satisfaction of his elders. Yet today this lad, now an adolescent who has plenty of money at his disposal and the freedom to buy up all the sweetmeats of the Viennese confectionery shops, is not able to eat a piece of chocolate without blushing furiously. Everybody who observes him is at once certain that he is doing something forbidden —that he is eating things bought with stolen money. You notice that the restrictions imposed upon him earlier have not automatically yielded to the changed situation.

Listen again to another example, this time not so harmless. A boy loves his mother with special tenderness; all his desires are directed toward filling the place which actually belongs to his father, and toward being her confidant and protector and her best-beloved. The child now suffers repeatedly the devastating experience that his father is the rightful owner of the position for which he is striving. It is his father who has the power to send him away from his mother at any time and to show him his own childish helplessness and impotence. The prohibition to aspire to his father's place is strengthened by his own fear of the father's great potency. Later, when he is an adolescent, this boy evinces a tormenting timidity and uncertainty which he feels as an unbearable obstacle when he finds himself in the same house as the girl he loves. The basis of his fear is that somebody may come and declare that the place he is occupying belongs to another and he has no right to it. To avoid this extremely painful situation he employs a great deal of his energy in preparing excuses which could plausibly explain to this other person his presence there.

Or take another case. A tiny little girl develops an extreme pleasure in her naked body, shows herself naked to her brothers and sisters, and delights in running through the rooms stark naked before she goes to bed. Education steps in and again with success. The little girl now makes a very great effort to suppress this desire. The result is an intense feeling of modesty that continues in later life. When the question of choosing a career arises somebody suggests an occupation which would necessitate sharing a room with companions. She unhesitatingly states that this career is not for her. Behind the rational motive the fear is ultimately revealed that she will have to undress before the others. The question of qualification or preference for the career is of no consequence compared with the strength of the prohibition carried over from childhood.

The psychoanalyst who is engaged in his

therapeutic work of "resolving" such inhibitions and disturbances in development certainly learns to know education from its worst side. Here, he feels, they have been shooting at sparrows with cannon balls! Would it not have been better perhaps to have given somewhat less value to decorum and convention in these various nurseries, and to have let the first child be greedy and the second imagine himself in the role of the father; to have permitted the third child to run about naked and a fourth to play with his genitals? Would these childish gratifications really have had any important adverse effect as compared with the damage wrought by a so-called "good education"? Compare them with the division which is thus introduced into the childish personality; the way in which one part of him is incited against another; see how the capacity to love is diminished and the child grows up incapable, perhaps, of enjoyment and of accomplishing his life-work. The analyst to whom all this is apparent resolves, so far as he is concerned, not to aid such an education, but to leave his own children free rather than to educate in this way. He would rather risk the chance of their being somewhat uncontrolled in the end instead of forcing on them from the outset such a crippling of their individuality.

But you are, I feel sure, shocked at the onesidedness of my views. It is high time to change the standpoint. Education appears to us in another light when we have another aim in view—for example, when it is concerned with the neglected child, such as August Aichhorn deals with in his book *Neglected Youth*.

The neglected child, says Aichhorn, refuses to take his place in society. He cannot succeed in controlling his instinctive impulses; he cannot divert enough energy from his sexual instincts to employ them for purposes more highly esteemed by society. He refuses, therefore, to submit to the restrictions which are binding on the society in which he lives, and equally withdraws from any participation in its life and work. No one who has had to do with this type of child in an educational or psychoanalytical connection can fail to regret that in his childhood there had been no force from without which succeeded in restricting his instinctual life, so that these external checks would have been gradually transformed into inner restrictions.

Take as an example a child who for a little while occupied the attention of the Vienna Children's Court. This eight-year-old girl was equally impossible both at home and at school. From every educational institute or convalescent home she was unhesitatingly sent back to her parents, after three days at the most. She refused to learn anything or to share in the activities of the other children. She pretended to be stupid, and so cleverly that in several places she was diagnosed as mentally defective. During the lessons she lay down on a bench and played with her sexual parts. Any interruption of this occupation resulted in a wild howling horrifying to the grownups. At home she was ill-treated—this was the only idea the parents had of dealing with her. An analytic investigation showed two things. The external circumstances were peculiarly unfavorable to the development of any kind of emotional relations between the child and her environment. No one could offer a love that would have in any way compensated the child for giving up the gratification obtained from her own body. It also showed that the severe punishments from which the parents had obviously expected a restraining influence could not fulfill this purpose. Either owing to her own disposition or on account of significant early experience, the little girl had developed such strong masochistic tendencies that each beating could only become once more a stimulus to sex excitement and sex activity. Compare this case of neglect with the one of repression which I described to you earlier. You can see that a free and self-reliant human being does not evolve from this child either. She is nothing but a cowed little animal whose further moral development has stopped simultaneously with her mental growth.

Aichhorn mentions in his book *Neglected Youth* another severe case of maldevelopment —that of a boy who from about his sixth year onward had found every kind of sexual gratification in his mother, and finally, after reaching sexual maturity, lived with her in actual sexual intercourse. He had thus actually accomplished what the other children had enjoyed only in fantasy. Neither has this boy developed into a self-reliant, harmonious, vigorous human being, as we might have expected, considering the evil effects of education described above.

A kind of "short-circuiting" had occurred in his development. By the actual fulfillment of his childhood's wishes he had saved himself the necessity of traversing the whole circle of "becoming grown-up." The wish to become like his father in order to attain all the possibilities of the gratifications permitted to his father was now superfluous. He had indeed escaped the "splitting" of his personality, but in return for that he had given up any further development.

But you will find that the problem is not so difficult as I have represented it to you, and that disturbances in development and delinquency may be merely extreme results, showing, on the one hand, the injurious effect of too great repression, on the other the lack of all restraint. The task of a pedagogy based

upon analytic data is to find a *via media* between these extremes—that is to say, to allow
to each stage in the child's life the right pro-
portion of instinct-gratification and instinct-
restriction.

Possibly a detailed description of this new
analytical pedagogy should have been the content of my lectures to you. But for the present
no analytical pedagogy exists. We have only
as yet individual educators who are interested
in this work, and having been analyzed themselves they now seek to apply to the education
of children the understanding that psychoanalysis has brought to them of their own instinctual life. It will be a long time before
theory and practice are complete and can be
recommended for general use.

But in spite of this you ought not to say
that psychoanalysis has done nothing beyond
giving indications as to the future; that it certainly does not profit teachers engaged in
practical work to study psychoanalysis, and
that probably it would be better to dissuade
them from having anything to do with it. Nor
should you say that they had better make en-

quiries in ten or twenty years' time as to what has been accomplished meanwhile in the application of psychoanalysis to pedagogics.

I maintain that even today psychoanalysis does three things for pedagogy. In the first place, it is well qualified to offer a criticism of existing educational methods. In the second place, the teacher's knowledge of human beings is extended, and his understanding of the complicated relations between the child and the educator is sharpened by psychoanalysis, which gives us a scientific theory of the instincts, of the unconscious and of the libido. Finally, as a method of practical treatment, in the analysis of children, it endeavors to repair the injuries which are inflicted upon the child during the processes of education.

The following example illustrates the second point, i.e. it explains the pedagogical situation by means of the unconscious background of the conscious behavior.

An excellent woman teacher began her career in her eighteenth year when, in consequence of unhappy family circumstances, she left home to take a post as governess to three boys. The second boy presented a serious educational problem. He was backward in his lessons and appeared very timid, reserved, and dull; he played a subordinate part in the family, and in contrast to his two gifted and attractive brothers was constantly pushed into the background. The teacher devoted all her efforts and interest to this boy, and in a comparatively short time had obtained a wonderful success.

The boy got very fond of her, was more devoted to her than he had ever been to anybody before, and became frank and friendly in his ways. His interest in lessons increased, and by her efforts she succeeded in teaching him in one year the subjects laid down for two years, so that he was no longer behind in his work. The parents were now proud of this child, whom until then they had treated with but slight affection; they took much more trouble about him, and his relations to them and also to his brothers improved, until the little boy was finally accepted as a most valued member of the family circle. Thereupon an unexpected difficulty arose. The teacher to whom the success was entirely due began now on her side to have trouble with the boy. She no longer gave him any love, and could not get on with him. Finally, she left the house, where she was greatly appreciated, on account of the very child who had been in the beginning the center of attraction to her.

The psychoanalytic treatment which she underwent nearly fifteen years later for pedagogic reasons revealed to her the true facts of the case. In her own home, as a child, she had, with more or less justification, imagined herself the unloved child—the same position in which she had actually found the second boy when she began her work with him. On the ground of similar slighting treatment she had seen herself in this boy, and had identified herself with him. All the love and care which she had lavished upon him meant that she was really saying to herself: "That is the way I ought to have been treated to make something out of me." Success, when it came, destroyed this identification. It made the pupil an independent being who could no longer be identified with her own life. The hostile feelings toward him arose from envy; she could not help grudging him the success which she herself had never attained.

You will say, perhaps, it was a good thing that this teacher, when she dealt with her pupil, had not yet been analyzed; otherwise we should have lost a fine educational success. But I feel that these educational successes are too dearly bought. They are paid for by the failures with those children who are not fortunate enough to reveal symptoms of suffering which remind the teacher of her own childhood and so make sympathy with them possible for her. I hold we are right in demanding that the teacher or educator should have learned to know and to control his own conflicts before he begins his educational work. If this is not so, the pupils merely serve as more or less suitable material on which to abreact his own unconscious and unsolved difficulties.

But in addition, the manifest behavior of the child is very seldom sufficient ground for a correct judgment. I will now give you the following notes which a boy dictated as the first chapter of an extensive book. As is so often the case with children, it remained a fragment.

"CHAPTER I

"THE WRONG THINGS
GROWN-UP PEOPLE DO

"Here, you grown-up people, listen to me, if you want to know something! Don't be too cocky and imagine that children can't do everything that grown-up people do. But they can do most of what you do. But children will never obey if you order them about like this, for example: 'Now, go and undress, quick's the word, get along.' Then they will never undress, don't you believe it. But when you speak nicely, then they will do it at once. You think you can do all you want to do, but don't imagine any such thing. And don't ever say: 'You must do this, you "must" do that!' No one 'must' do things, neither therefore 'must' children do things. You think children 'must' wash themselves. Certainly not. Then you say, 'But if you don't wash, everybody will say "Oh fie, how dirty he is!" and so you "must" wash yourself.' No, he 'mustn't,' but he does wash, so that people won't call him dirty.

"When you tell children what they are to do that's enough, and don't tell them so much about how they are to do it, for they do what they think right, just as you do. And don't always say to them, 'You "mustn't" buy such and such a thing,' for if they pay for it themselves they can buy what they like. Don't always say to children, 'You can't do that!' For they can do many things better than you, and you won't ever believe it, and afterwards you are astonished. Don't always talk so much; let the children sometimes get a word in!"

Now, suppose these written remarks were found in a school and taken to the head master. He would say to himself that this was a dangerous boy on whom one must keep one's eye. From further enquiry he would find out still more serious things about him. The boy was in the habit of making blasphemous remarks about God; he described the priests in language that can scarcely be repeated; he strongly urged his companions not to put up with any interference, and indeed he even planned to go into the zoological gardens and set free the animals whom he regarded as wrongfully imprisoned there. Now a conservative teacher of the old school would say: The rebellious spirit of this boy must be broken by some means or other before it is too late and he has become a serious menace to society. A modern educator, on the contrary, would have the highest hopes of this child's future, and would expect to see in him a future leader and liberator of the masses.

I must tell you that both teachers would be wrong, and all methods of training which they might base upon their knowledge of the manifest situation would be harmful and false. The eight-year-old boy is a harmless little coward, who is in terror when a dog barks at him, who is frightened to go along the dark passage in the evening, and certainly would not be capable of injuring a fly. His rebellious savings come about in the following way. His early passionate emotional relations, accompanied by an intense preoccupation with his penis, were destroyed as the result of education and of medical treatment from which he experienced severe shock. As a safeguard against new temptations there remained an immense fear, that of being punished on the guilty part of his body, the fear which psychoanalysis names *castration-fear*. This fear caused him now to deny any kind of authority. When anybody has power, he says to himself, then he has the power to punish me. Consequently every possibility of a heavenly or earthly ruler must be removed from the world. The greater his fear of temptation the more he seeks to drown it by his quite harmless attacks on those in authority. This noisy method of protecting himself is, moreover, not his only one. Although he acts the part of an atheist, he kneels down in the evening and prays, secretly impelled by fear. He thinks: "There is indeed no God. But perhaps after all there might be one, and then it would be a good thing, in any case, to behave properly to Him." Now I take it this boy will become neither a menace to society nor a liberator of the masses. What he needs is, indeed, neither admiration of his efforts nor harshness and restrictions, but only—by some means or other —an abatement of his fear which will enable him, released now from his neurotic way of living, to obtain later on the capacity for enjoyment and work.

The psychoanalytic method of treatment which can achieve this is, then, the third service that psychoanalysis has rendered to education. But the description of this method, namely, child analysis, would go far beyond the limits of this course.

Index

Horney, Karen. *Our Inner Conflicts.*

Horney, Karen. *Self-Analysis*

Inhelder, Bärbel, and Jean Piaget. *The Early Growth of Logic in the Child.*

James, William. *Talks to Teachers.*

Kagan, Jerome, and Robert Coles (Eds.). *Twelve to Sixteen: Early Adolescence.*

Kasanin, J. S. *Language and Thought in Schizophrenia.*

Kelly, George A. *A Theory of Personality.*

Klein, Melanie, and Joan Riviere. *Love, Hate and Reparation.*

Komarovsky, Mirra. *Dilemmas of Masculinity: A Study of College Youth.*

Lasswell, Harold D. *Power and Personality.*

Levy, David M. *Maternal Overprotection.*

Lifton, Robert Jay *Revolutionary Immortality: Mao Tse-tung and the Chinese Cultural Revolution.*

Lifton, Robert Jay *Thought Reform and the Psychology of Totalism.*

Meehl, Paul E. *Psychodiagnosis: Selected Papers.*

Piaget, Jean. *The Child's Conception of Number.*

Piaget, Jean *Genetic Epistemology.*

Piaget, Jean. *Play, Dreams and Imitation in Childhood.*

Piaget, Jean. *Understanding Causality.*

Piaget, Jean, and Bärbel Inhelder. *The Child's Conception of Space.*

Piaget, Jean, and Bärbel Inhelder. *The Origin of the Idea of Chance in Children.*

Piers, Gerhart, and Milton B. Singer. *Shame and Guilt.*

Piers, Maria W. (Ed.). *Play and Development.*

Raymond, Margaret, Andrew Slaby, and Julian Lieb. *The Healing Alliance.*

Ruesch, Jurgen. *Disturbed Communication.*

Ruesch, Jurgen. *Therapeutic Communication.*

Ruesch, Jurgen, and Gregory Bateson. *Communication: The Social Matrix of Psychiatry.*

Sullivan, Harry Stack. *Clinical Studies in Psychiatry.*

Sullivan, Harry Stack. *Conceptions of Modern Psychiatry.*

Sullivan, Harry Stack. *The Fusion of Psychiatry and Social Science.*

Sullivan, Harry Stack. *The Interpersonal Theory of Psychiatry.*

Sullivan, Harry Stack. *The Psychiatric Interview.*

Sullivan, Harry Stack. *Schizophrenia as a Human Process.*

Walter, W. Grey. *The Living Brain.*

Watson, John B. *Behaviorism.*

Wheelis, Allen. *The Quest for Identity.*

Williams, Juanita H. *Psychology of Women: Behavior in a Biosocial Context.*

Zilboorg, Gregory. *A History of Medical Psychology.*